Each Day is a Miracle

Gina Cronrath

WestBow Press books may be ordered through booksellers or by contacting:

WestBow Press
A Division of Thomas Nelson & Zondervan
1663 Liberty Drive
Bloomington, IN 47403
www.westbowpress.com
844-714-3454

ISBN: 978-1-6642-8653-5 (sc)
ISBN: 978-1-6642-8668-9 (e)

Library of Congress Control Number: 2022923068

Print information available on the last page.

WestBow Press rev. date: 12/09/2022

WESTBOW
PRESS®
A DIVISION OF THOMAS NELSON
& ZONDERVAN

Each Day is a Miracle

When I wake up in the morning

Feel the warm sun on my skin

I know another miracle day
is about to begin.

2

Some miracles are big, others small

All of them are special

God's Blessings to us all.

Holding a cuddly, soft puppy,

Watching the flowers grow,

Eating chocolate ice cream,

These are all miracles I know.

Being a friend to someone
who feels alone,

The miracle of love
is being shown.

Helping a child cross
the street,

Showing kindness to
everyone we meet.

A kind word spoken,

A friendly smile to
one another,

Giving a hug

To brother, sister,
father, and mother.

At the end of the day,

With the moon shining bright,

Crawling into bed and
saying good- night,

We look up to the Heavens
and lovingly say,

"Thank-you God for your
miracles today."

Printed in the United States
by Baker & Taylor Publisher Services